TEACHINGS OF THE EARTH

D0732793

DHARMA COMMUNICATIONS BOOKS BY JOHN DAIDO LOORI

TEACHINGS OF THE EARTH

ZEN AND THE ENVIRONMENT

John Daido Loori

SHAMBHALA • BOSTON & LONDON • 2007

Shambhala Publications, Inc.
Horticultural Hall
300 Massachusetts Avenue
Boston, Massachusetts 02115
www.shambhala.com

9 8 7 6 5 4 3 2 1
First Shambhala Edition
Printed in the United States of America

♾ This edition is printed on acid-free paper that meets the
American National Standards Institute z39.48 Standard.
Distributed in the United States by Random House, Inc.,
and in Canada by Random House of Canada Ltd

Designed by Margery Cantor

Library of Congress Cataloging-in-Publication Data
Loori, John Daido.
[Teachings of the insentient]
Teachings of the earth: Zen and the environment /
text and photographs by John Daido Loori.
p.   cm.
Originally published: Teachings of the insentient.
Mt. Tremper, NY: Dharma Communications, 1999.
ISBN 978-1-59030-490-7 (pbk.: alk. paper)
1. Human ecology—Religious aspects—Zen Buddhism. 2. Nature—
Religious aspects—Zen Buddhism. 3. Zen Buddhism—Doctrines. I. Title.
BQ9268.6.L66 2007
294.3'377—dc22
2007020397

I swear the earth shall surely be complete
     to him or her who shall be complete,
The earth remains jagged and broken
     only to him or her who remains jagged or broken

—WALT WHITMAN

CONTENTS

PREFACE

IMAGINE, IF YOU WILL, a universe in which all things have a mutual identity. They all have an interdependent origination: when one thing arises, all things arise simultaneously. And everything has a mutual causality: what happens to one thing happens to the entire universe. Imagine a universe that is a self-creating, self-maintaining, and self-defining organism—a universe in which all the parts and the totality are a single entity; all of the pieces and the whole thing are, at once, one thing.

This description of reality is not a holistic hypothesis or an idealistic dream. It is your life and my life, the life of the mountain and the life of the river, the life of a blade of grass, a spiderweb, the Brooklyn Bridge. These things are not related to each other. They're not part of the same thing.

They're not similar. Rather, they are identical to each other in every respect.

But the way we live our lives is as if that were not so. We live in a way that separates the pieces, alienates and hurts. The Buddhist teachings offered in this book point to how we can live our lives in harmony with the facts described above. These teachings refer to us and the whole universe, and we need to see them and practice them from that perspective if we are to benefit from what they have to offer, and begin healing the rift between ourselves and the universe.

To practice Zen is to be in harmony with your life and the universe. To practice Zen means to study the self exhaustively—not just on the surface but on many levels, plumbing its depths. It means being deeply honest with yourself. It means taking responsibility for your life. If you don't practice taking responsibility for your life, you are not practicing Zen. It is as simple as that.

To take responsibility empowers you to do something about whatever it is that's hindering you. As long as we blame, as long as we avoid or deny, we are removed from the realm of possibility and power to do something about our lives. We become totally dependent upon the ups and downs that we create around us. There is no reason that we should be subjected to anything when we have the power to see that we create and we destroy all things. To acknowledge that simple fact is to take possession of your life. It is to make these teachings your own. It is to give life to the Buddha, to this great earth, and to the universe itself.

—John Daido Loori, Abbot
Zen Mountain Monastery

TEACHINGS OF THE EARTH

BORN AS THE EARTH

THE TEACHINGS OF the buddhadharma about our relationship to the natural environment are far ahead of the world's scientific understanding. In general, our ecology is based on separation. The teachings, on the other hand, are about intimacy. The way we view ourselves and the way we view the ten thousand things is the fundamental matter that makes all the difference in how we live our lives and how we relate to all of the so-called externals.

In engaging Zen training with an eye on its relationship to ecological concerns, we ask the question, "Where does the earth end and where do I begin?" We study the practice of survival: survival in and of the mountains, the forests, the rivers, the cities; survival of the individual and of the human species, of the community and the family, and, indeed, survival of this great earth itself. It's a very important teaching, the teaching of the insentient. Given technological developments and the fragile state of affairs on earth, a lot of wisdom and compassion are needed.

Being born as the earth is not the same as being born. It is not about birth. It is not about coming into the world. It is not a matter of occupying time or space. It is beyond time or space. Being born as the earth is to realize the world, period. To realize the mountains, the rivers, and the great earth as the body and mind of the Tathagata. Tathagata is at once the name of the Buddha and the word that's used to describe suchness, this very moment, right-here-and-now, and to realize one's own body and mind.

Dew on the pine, the grasses, and trees are the real form of truth. They are the limitless life of the endless spring. *Endless spring* is used in Buddhist text to refer to enlightenment or realization. The question is, Where do you find yourself?

A while ago an incident took place at Zen Mountain Monastery that points to the heart of this question. During an informal question-and-answer period a visiting student started to recite a poem of Walt Whitman to illustrate a point he wanted to make. He quoted, "The truths of the earth continually wait. They are not so concealed either. They are calm, subtle, untransmissible by print." I challenged him, asking, "Those are the words that described this reality. What is the reality itself? Show me." He was unable to respond.

As far as I know, Whitman was not a Buddhist. He probably never even read anything about Buddhism. But there is no question in my mind that he was realized. Once in a while any poet will walk on water, but Whitman was on water all the time. Even his inconsistencies are consistent. This is the poem that the student was quoting:

The earth does not withhold, it is generous
  enough.
The truths of the earth continually wait,
  they are not so conceal'd either,
They are calm, subtle, untransmissible by print,
They are imbued through all things,
  conveying themselves willingly . . .

The earth does not argue,
Is not pathetic, has no arrangements,
Does not scream, haste, persuade, threaten,
  promise,

Makes no discriminations,
*   has no conceivable failures,*
Closes nothing, refuses nothing, shuts none out.
Of all the powers, objects, states,
*   it notifies, shuts none out.*

What a wonderful way of being—and it is the potential of all sentient beings, every one of us, not just of the earth itself.

Whitman begins a poem called "The Song of the Rolling Earth" by saying:

A song of the rolling earth, and of words
*   according,*
Were you thinking that those were the words,
*   those upright lines, those curves, angles, dots?*
No, those are not the words, the substantial
*   words are in the ground and sea,*
They are in the air, they are in you.

Were you thinking that those were the words,
*   those delicious sounds out of your friends'*
*   mouths?*
No, the real words are more delicious than they.

Human bodies are words, myriads of words,
(In the best poems re-appears the body,
man's or woman's, well-shaped, natural, gay,
Every part able, active, receptive
without shame or the need of shame.)

Air, soil, water, fire—those are words,
I myself am a word with them—
my qualities interpenetrate with theirs.

It seems he understood that the words and ideas that describe reality are not the same as the reality itself, and that each one of us needs to realize it for ourselves. No one can do it for us. He says:

Whoever you are! motion and reflection
*   are especially for you,*
The divine ship sails the divine sea, for you.
Whoever you are! you are he or she for whom
*   the earth is solid and liquid,*
You are he or she for whom
*   the sun and moon hang in the sky,*

For none more than you are the present and
     the past,
For none more than you is immortality.
Each man to himself and each woman to
     herself,
  is the word of the past and the present,
  and the true word of immortality;
No one can aquire it for another—not one,
No one can grow for another—not one.

These could have been the words of the Buddha, Master Dogen, Han-shan, Tung-shan. We've
heard them so many times—not nearly so elo-
quently, but of course this was written in our lan-
guage; the others were translated, sometimes two
or three times. But isn't it remarkable? I don't
know if Whitman knew anything about formal
zazen. I can find nothing in his biographies or his
writings that indicates any *kensho* experience, but
I am certain he has seen it. You can't fake something like this. There are poets who, because of a
particular experience at one moment in time, can
write something extraordinary. But then you see

in other parts of their work that the clarity is not consistently there. It was just a momentary insight. But Whitman's vision is continual. You can open up almost any page of *Leaves of Grass*, let your eyes fall on any line, and there it is, again and again.

What a shame to take this beautiful insight and tie it up, frame it, with words and ideas. Our tendency is to think that when we can name something, fit it into our reference system, and describe it, then we understand it. This is largely how our academic education functions. This is how we make it through college and, quite often, this is how we attempt to get through life. We regurgitate what we've swallowed. That rote playback is too frequently regarded as the actual test of understanding. How do we go beyond that? How do we go beyond the words and ideas that describe reality and directly experience the reality itself? We spend a lifetime honing and perfecting the aspect of consciousness that is linear and sequential. Overpowered by words, ideas, positions, and understanding, the intuitive aspect of human consciousness is all but forgotten. But when the mind settles down and we stop talking to ourselves, this

aspect of consciousness begins to open up. And nature is a wonderful place for that to happen. Nature is not logical. It's not predictable. It's not really understandable. We can categorize and analyze it, but that is not what nature is really about. A description of nature is no more the thing itself than descriptions of ourselves are what the self really is.

The whole point of Zen training in a natural environment is to make us open and receptive to the insentient, to nature itself as the teacher. Being born as the earth is about intimacy. It is about wholeness and completeness. We tend to fragment ourselves. We tend to be our own worst enemies, all of us. And it's got to do with our internalized program, the program of the biocomputer, our conditioning. The way we respond to circumstances, the way we see ourselves, is all learned behavior. It took training to put it there. That's why the process of zazen is so necessary. Layer by layer we need to deal with that conditioning. Layer by layer, we peel it back, examining it, understanding it clearly, throwing it away, and going deeper. Layer by layer until finally we reach the ground of being, and that too needs to be seen, and then thrown away. We just keep going. Zen practice is an endless process. And what it is about is really seeing the wholeness. First we see it within ourselves, then we see it in accord with the ten thousand things.

Again Whitman:

I swear the earth shall surely be complete
  to him or her who shall be complete,
The earth remains jagged and broken
  only to him or her who remains jagged
    and broken
I swear, there is no greatness of power
  that does not emulate those of the earth,
there can be no theory of any account
  unless it corroborate the theory of the earth,
No politics, song, religion, behavior, or what not,
  is of account unless it compare
  with the amplitude of the earth,

Unless it face the exactness, vitality,
    impartiality,
  rectitude of the earth.

I swear I begin to see love with sweeter
        spasms than
    that which responds love,
It is that which contains itself,
    which never invites and never refuses.
I swear
I begin to see little or nothing in audible words,
All merges toward the presentation
    of the unspoken meanings of the earth,
Toward him who sings the songs
    of the body and of the truths of the earth,
Toward him who makes the dictionaries
    of words that print cannot touch.

With the gift of life comes the possibility of pain and anguish. With it also comes the possibility of great peace and harmony. How it turns out is up to you. It is clear that we haven't really bought into the description of reality passed onto us by our conditioning. Intuitively we sense that there must be more to it than we've been told. More to it than the philosophers and the priests and the politicians tell us. Well, we're right. There is. But there isn't a soul on the face of this great earth

who can give it to us or do it for us. It is also true
that once you have made up your mind to do it,
and really put yourself into it, you will do it. If your
effort is sincere, if you are honest with yourself,
you will do it. No beings ever come short of their
own completeness. No beings ever fail to cover
the ground on which they stand.

But it is not easy. The self is programmed not
to be forgotten. You sit there trying to forget the
self—and just the trying recreates, from moment
to moment, the self. All kinds of barriers come up.
Every time you get to that edge of "falling away of
body and mind," something pulls you back. That is
the program. "I'm here, I'm here, I'm here—you're
there." In a sense, that strong ego, that strong sense
of self and separateness that has been part of the
process of evolution, is how we have survived as a
species. We are not as fast as the other animals,
nor as agile. We can't fly. We're not as strong as
they are. All we have is our intellect, our wit. And
Big Ego. Our intellect has now developed to the
point where it threatens to extinguish the species
itself. We've created a world that puts us on the
threshold of life and death as a species. When that

kind of power is in the hands of leaders convinced that who they are is the bag of skin and everything else is the rest of the universe, we have a dangerous situation. On the other hand, if you realize the earth, and are intimate with the ten thousand things, then there is no need for an Environmental Protection Agency, or for any protective legislation whatsoever. If you realize the earth, then there is no need for the Buddhist precepts. There is no way, having once realized the earth, that we could live our lives in the old way.

But not everybody is going to realize it, at least not for many lifetimes. And those of us who are lucky enough to find our way into this incredible dharma have a responsibility to use its wisdom and sense of intimacy in a way that nourishes the earth itself and all its inhabitants. In a sense it's a very selfish thing, in that what you do to the earth, you do to yourself. What you do to the smallest thing on this great earth, you do to all of it. Cause and effect are one reality.

It is no small thing to be born human. With it comes a tremendous responsibility. That responsibility is due to our intelligence, our awareness. We have the power, each of us, not only to change our own lives and bring them into harmony with the ten thousand things, but also to nourish others, to heal this planet. The harmony, nourishment, and healing are within the capabilities of the same science and technology that have created the destruction. We can do it. All it takes is the will to do it. You can realize yourself; all it takes is the determination to do it. In both cases, we're fully equipped. We have everything needed to realize ourselves and transform our lives, and to realize the earth and transform this planet. As always, it is up to you. What will you do with the opportunity? When will you do it? Please, don't waste this precious life.

– Cause + effect

TEACHINGS OF THE INSENTIENT

WE ARE IN a unique period of human history. For the first time, the major threats to our existence are not the natural disasters that were the biggest fears for our predecessors a thousand years ago, but human-created dangers. This places us at a critical time in evolution, a time that could decide the fate of both the human race and the planet we all share. The most compelling paradox we are encountering is that, on the one hand, we possess a degree of knowledge and technological capability hardly dreamed of only decades ago. We understand complex data about the furthest reaches of space and the most subtle workings of minute fragments of atoms. On the other hand, millions of us starve. Our enviroment is polluted. The earth's natural resources are being plundered at an alarming rate, and the spectre of global ecological catastrophe raises the possibility of the extinction of our species and all life. In spite of our understanding so much about the universe and its functioning, we've barely begun to scratch the surface of understanding who we are, what our life is, and what our relationship is with the "ten thousand things" that comprise phenomenal existence.

Our way of perceiving ourselves and the universe has remained dualistic and virtually static throughout the development of human history. It is a perspective that assumes separation of self and other. As a result of that assumption of duality, we've created forms of philosophy, art, science, medicine, ecology, theology, psychology, politics, sociology, ethics, and morality that are basically permutations derived from that initial premise of separation. The emerging consequences create the kind of world we now live in. The issues of nuclear war, pollution of natural resources, the AIDS epidemic, the national drug problem, poverty, starvation, and immorality in religion, politics, and business all share the fundamental idea of how we understand the self. How we understand the self is how we understand the universe, and how we understand the universe determines how we relate to it, what we do about it, and how we combust our lives within it.

Very recently in the West, we've become aware of the existence of an entirely different way of understanding reality. Its origins go back to a piece of writing once known only to Buddhists. In the *Flower Garland Sutra,* composed in seventh-century China, a universe is described in which everything interpenetrates with everything else in identity and interdependence; in which everything needs everything else and there's not a single speck of dust that does not affect the whole. In the sutra's most resounding metaphor, the Diamond Net of Indra, all existence is seen as a vast net of gems that extends throughout the universe, not only in the three dimensions of space but in the fourth dimension of time as well. Each point of this huge net contains a multifaceted diamond which reflects every other diamond, and as such, essentially "contains" every other diamond in the net. The diamonds represent the entire universe of the past, present, and future. In a sense, what the metaphor depicts is how each and every thing in the universe contains every other thing throughout all time.

The Diamond Net of Indra is not just a philosophical postulation; it is a description of realized reality. It is the direct experience of thousands of Buddhist men and women for more than two thousand years. Predictably, not too many people took this teaching very seriously until the twentieth century, when the discovery of one of the unique uses of laser light demonstrated the relevance of this ancient image. Using laser light you can make a photographic image on a photographic plate; when laser light is transmitted through the plate, a three-dimensional image is projected. This in itself is pretty remarkable—a holographic image you can walk into, that allows you to actually sit among the objects in the picture. Even more remarkable, and what is radically changing our basic way of seeing things, is the fact that you can cut that photographic plate in half and project laser light through only half of it and still project the whole image. You can cut the half in half and project through it and still project the whole image, cut the quarter in half, cut the eighth in half and so on, down to the smallest piece of that photographic plate. When you project light through it, you project the whole image. Nothing is missing. This indicates only one thing: each part of the plate contains all the information of the whole, just like the gems in the Diamond Net.

TEACHINGS OF THE INSENTIENT
limited conditioning

As a result of that discovery, biologists have begun to examine biology in terms of the holographic model. New brain theory also uses a holographic model, and physicists have begun to look at the universe through the "eyes" of a holographic paradigm. Now in the twenty-first century, scientists are beginning to provide experimental verification of the experience transmitted as the Diamond Net for 2,500 years by Buddhist practitioners.

Realizing the holographic universe is what I like to call twenty-first century mind because it's only by coming to understand the nature of the universe as a whole that there is any possibility of doing something about the problems we face. Twenty-first century mind is the mind of ancient buddhas; it's the buddha mind, the mind of all sentient beings. We already have it, but we've buried it under a lifetime of conditioning—conditioning by our parents, teachers, culture, nation, and education. When we realize the interdependent universe, there's no way to avoid responsibility for it; it becomes unavoidably clear that what we do and what happens to us are the same thing. When you realize that deeply, it's no longer possible to postpone, blame, or be a victim. We create our universe—that's what is realized. That is the empowerment that comes from realization. When we listen to the problems of the world, it's easy to be overwhelmed by a feeling of despair. What can we do? The situation seems hopeless. Out of that despair and hopelessness can come a true empowerment, but that will only become real for us when we understand who we really are—beyond the bag of skin, beyond the words and ideas that describe ourselves. What is the truth, the reality of our existence? What is "beingness" itself?

At a very young age, in T'ang Dynasty China, Zen Master Tung-shan was asking such probing questions. Upon hearing the line in the *Heart Sutra*, "No eye, ear, nose, tongue, body, mind," he touched his face and said, "I have eyes, ears, and nose. Why does the scripture say they don't exist?" Practitioners have been chanting the *Heart Sutra* at this Monastery for almost twenty years, and thousands of different people have stood in the zendo and intoned "No eye, ear, nose, tongue, body, mind. No color, sound, smell, taste, touch, phenomena. No world of sight, no world of consciousness." Yet I can count on one hand the number of students who asked the question this ten-year-old child asked his teacher. "Why does it say that? I *have* them." Tung-shan's teacher couldn't answer and directed him to a Zen master under whom he became ordained as a monastic when he was twenty-one years old.

Once, near the beginning of his study, Tung-shan was at the monastery of the great Master Nan-ch'üan on the anniversary of the death of Ma-tsu, who had been Nan-ch'üan's teacher. As they were preparing a memorial service, Nan-ch'üan asked the group of students, "We're having a memorial service for Ma-tsu tomorrow. Do you think he'll come?" At first nobody answered. Then the young monastic Tung-shan came forward and said, "He'll come when he has a companion." Nan-ch'üan said, "Although this is a young man, he is suitable for cutting and polishing." Tung-shan said, "Don't demean the good," and walked away.

Next, Tung-shan called on Master Kuei-shan, and asked, "Recently I heard that the National

Teacher had a saying about the teaching of insentient beings. I don't understand the subtle meaning." Kuei-shan said, "Do you remember it?" Tung-shan said, "Yes." Kuei-shan said, "Say it." Tung-shan said, "A monastic asked, 'What is the mind of the ancient buddhas?' The teacher said, 'Fences, walls, tiles, pebbles.' The monastic said, 'Aren't those inanimate things?' The teacher said, 'Yes.' The monastic said, 'Can they teach?' The teacher said, 'They're always teaching clearly and unceasingly.' The monastic said, 'Why can't I hear them?' The teacher said, 'You yourself don't hear but you shouldn't hinder that which does hear.' The monastic said, 'Who can hear it?' The teacher said, 'The sages can.' The monastic said, 'Do you hear it?' The teacher said, 'No.' The monastic said, 'If you don't hear it, how do you know insentient things can teach?' The teacher said, 'It's luck that I don't hear it, for if I did I'd be equal to the sages and you wouldn't hear my teaching.' The monastic said, 'Then living beings have no part in it?' The teacher said, 'I teach for the sake of living beings, not for the saints and sages.' The monastic said, 'After sentient beings hear it, then what?' The teacher said, 'Then they're not sentient beings.' The monastic said, 'What scripture is the teaching of the inanimate based on?' The teacher said, 'Obviously words that do not accord with the classics are not the talk of a scholar. Haven't you read the *Flower Garland Sutra?* It says that lands teach, beings teach, all things and all times teach.'"

After Tung-shan had recited this story, Kuei-shan said, "I also have it here, but I hardly ever meet anyone suitable for it." Tung-shan said, "I don't understand. Please teach me." Kuei-shan held up the whisk and asked, "Understand?" Tung-shan said, "I don't." Kuei-shan said, "Words will never explain it to you." Tung-shan asked, "Is there anyone who can help me?" Kuei-shan directed him to Master Yün-yen.

Tung-shan left Kuei-shan and went to Master Yün-yen. Bringing up the preceding question, he asked: "Who can hear the teaching of the insentient?" Yün-yen responded, "The insentients can hear it." Tung-shan said, "Why don't I hear it?" Yün-yen held up the fly whisk and said, "Do you hear?" Tung-shan said, "No." Yün-yen said, "If you don't even hear my teaching, how could you hear the teaching of the insentient?" Tung-shan said, "What scripture contains the teaching of the in-sentient?" Yün-yen said, "Haven't you read in the *Amitabha Sutra* where it says that rivers, birds, trees, and groves all invoke the Buddha and the teachings?" At this, Tung-shan had an awakening.

What is it that Tung-shan realized? Two dif-ferent teachers, two different lineages; same point, same teaching. What is the holding up of the whisk? The whisk referred to is a fly whisk, a small stick with horsehair on the end of it used to brush flies away without killing them. It became a sym-bol of the teaching, one of the things transmitted generation to generation. But it didn't matter that the whisk was something involved in the trans-mission; it was the holding up that revealed the teaching of the insentient. Raising the whisk, blinking the eyes, holding up the flower, calling and answering—all are concerned with intimacy. Intimacy is "seeing form with the whole body and mind, hearing sound with the whole body and mind." When you do that, you understand things intimately. That's what Tung-shan was experienc-ing, the teaching that can be derived from the ten

thousand things themselves. The very problems and barriers we face are the doorway to realization of the nature of the universe and the nature of the self.

How many ways can we say "intimacy?" We say that "no separation, no attachment" is intimacy. "No gain and no loss" is intimacy. "Cause and effect are one" is intimacy. "Responsibility" is intimacy. "Forget the self" is intimacy. "Really be yourself" is intimacy. All these are simply different ways of saying the same thing: be intimate. Yet so long as we lock ourselves into this bag of skin, we lock out the rest of the universe and there is no intimacy.

After expressing his understanding, Tung-shan said to Yün-yen, "I still have residual habits which have not yet been exhausted." Yün-yen said, "What have you done?" Tung-shan said, "I don't even practice the holy truths." In other words, no effort, no action, the action of non-action. Yün-yen said, "Are you happy?" Tung-shan said, "Yes. It's as though I've found a jewel in a trash heap." Then Tung-shan asked, "What should I do when I want to see my true being?" Yün-yen said, "Ask the messenger within." Tung-shan said, "I'm asking now." Yün-yen said, "What does he tell you?" The old man was trying to tell him: really trust yourself, have faith in yourself. The ten thousand things reduce to the self. The whole thing happens right here, in this very moment. As Tung-shan took leave of Yün-yen, he asked, "After your death, if someone asks me if I can describe your picture, how should I answer?" "Your picture" means "your teaching." In those days evidence of having received the transmission, was having a picture of your teacher. The picture had a double meaning: it also meant the teacher's reality, his teaching. Yün-yen remained silent for a while and then said, "It's just this." Tung-shan sank into thought. Yün-yen said, "You should be most thoroughgoing in your understanding of this matter."

Tung-shan still had some doubts; but later, upon seeing his reflection in the water while cross-ing a river, he was greatly enlightened to the meaning of what had transpired. He said in verse:

Don't seek it from others or
you'll estrange from yourself.

I now go out alone,
Everywhere I encounter it.
It now is me, I now am not it.
One must understand it in this way
to merge with being as it is.

Tung-shan's saying, "It now is me, I now am not it," has the same point as, "You and I are the same thing, yet I am not you and you are not me." Both sides of the statement exist simultaneously; it's not half of one side and half of the other, fifty-fifty. It's not a mixture. There is a unity beyond both that is neither absolute nor relative, neither up nor down, neither existing nor not existing. There is a reality that transcends all dualities, and the truth of this practice is to realize that. One of the difficulties with Zen practice is that people often put all of the attention on realizing the absolute basis of reality, and never complete the process. On the one hand we have the absolute basis in which there is "no eye, ear, nose, tongue, body, and mind." That is to be experienced. On the other hand we have the whole phenomenal universe. The truth is to be found in neither extreme. Sentient on one hand, insentient on the other. Secular on one hand, sacred on the other. Holy on one hand, profane on the other. Good, bad; man, woman; heaven, earth; up, down: all the dualities miss it. What is the truth that transcends them?

One of Tung-shan's great contributions is his formulation of the teaching called "The Five Ranks," depicting the integration of dualities. The first rank is "the relative within the absolute." This is emptiness—no eye, ear, nose, tongue, body, or mind. But there is no knowing it until we move to the next rank. The second rank is the realization of that emptiness, and is referred to as "the absolute within the relative." This is where the enlightenment experience, or *kensho*, happens. But still there is separation. Absolute and relative are still dualistic. The third rank is "coming from within the absolute." When you realize the whole universe as nothing but yourself, you have to take care of it. You have to be very selfish because that self is the ten thousand things, existing in the past, present, and future. Every action you take affects the totality of that universe. But understanding that doesn't impart much strength, because in understanding there is still separation between the knower and the thing the knower knows. Believing also doesn't impart strength—a belief system is usually dependent upon something else, and thus is vulnerable. But when you realize it you transform your life, and that transformation is empowering. No longer in the abstract, the whole matter becomes your very life itself and, inevitably, compassion begins to happen. You put your life on the line. There is just no way to avoid it when you realize that in fact your life is already on the line.

Tung-shan's fourth rank is "arriving at mutual integration," the coming from both absolute and relative. At this stage they are still two things; like a mixture of salt and pepper. There's integration, but in integration there are still two things. This is expressed with the image of the bodhisattva, who, face covered with dirt, descends the mountain and re-enters the marketplace. In the fifth rank, "unity attained," there is no longer a mixture. It is one thing—neither absolute nor relative, up nor down, profane nor holy, good nor bad, male nor female. What is it?

The same teaching on complete unity is presented by Master Dogen in his "Mountains and Rivers Sutra":

He who doubts that mountains walk does not yet understand his own walking. It's not that he doesn't walk, but that he doesn't yet understand, has not made clear his walking. They who would understand their own walking must also understand the walking of the blue mountains. The blue mountains are neither sentient nor insentient. The self is neither sentient nor insentient.

Master Keizan, commenting six hundred years later on Tung-shan's experiences, said,

So good people, observing carefully, you have become fully aware of this mystic consciousness. This is called insentient or inanimate. It is called inanimate because there is no running after sound and form, no bondage of emotion or discrimination. The National Teacher really explained this principle in detail, so when you hear talk of the insentient, don't make the mistake of understanding it as fences or walls. As long as your feelings and thoughts are not deluded and attached to your perception, and your perception is not scattered here and there at random, then that mystic consciousness will be bright and unclouded, clearly aware. If you try to grasp this, you cannot get it; it has no form, so it is not existent. If you try to get rid of it, you cannot separate from it because it is forever with you; it's not non-existent. It is not cognition, it is not thought, it is not tied to any of the psycho-physical elements. Then what is it?

When Keizan says there is "no bondage of emotion or discrimination" he does not mean lack of feeling or caring. He means no *bondage,* no attachment. What is no bondage to emotion? When you cry, just cry. When you feel, just feel with the whole body and mind. Don't separate yourself. Separation causes bondage, and separation inhibits and restricts our freedom.

This mystic teaching is always manifest and teaching clearly. It is what causes us to raise the eyebrows and blink the eyes. It is involved in our walking, standing, sitting, reclining, washing, hurrying, dying, being born, eating when hungry, sleeping when tired. All this is teaching, everything down to the chirping of insects. Nothing is hidden. Therefore, everything is always teaching clearly and unceasingly.

We should see and we should hear these teachings. We should see and hear the voice of these mountains and rivers, and of the endangered and extinct species. We should see and hear the voice of the atom, the homeless, the children; the voice of the teachings of countless generations past, present, and future. If you try to see with the eye and hear with the ear, you'll never get it. Only if you see with the ear and hear with the eye will you truly be able to see "it" clearly. How do you see with the ear and hear with the eye? Zazen. Zazen is the dragon entering the water, the lion entering the mountains. Zazen is the bodhi seat of the Buddha, the true transmission of the twenty-first century mind, the voice of the ten thousand things.

RIVER SEEING RIVER

Zen Master Dogen, writing in his "Mountains and Rivers Sutra," said:

The river is neither strong nor weak, neither wet nor dry, neither moving nor still, neither cold nor hot, neither being nor non-being, neither delusion nor enlightenment. Solidified, it is harder than diamond: who could break it? Melted, it is softer than milk: who could break it? This being the case we cannot doubt the many virtues realized by the river. We should then study that occasion, when the rivers of the ten directions are seen in the ten directions. This is not a study only of the time when humans and gods see the river: there is a study of the river seeing the river. The river practices and verifies the river; hence, there is a study of the river speaking river. We must bring to realization the path on which the self encounters the self. We must move back and forth along, and spring off from, the vital path on which the other studies and fully comprehends the other.

This section of the sutra has to do with the third of the Five Ranks of Master Tung-shan—a subtle and profound teaching which provides a matrix for, and a way of appreciating, the relative and absolute aspects of reality. The third rank reflects the development of maturity in practice— the functioning of emptiness in everyday life, the emergence of compassion as the activity of the world.

Dogen was a great lover of nature, an incredible poet and mystic. He built his monastery deep in the mountains on the Nine-Headed Dragon River. He did much of his work in a hermitage on the cliffs of the mountain. He was intimate with the mountains. But the mountains and rivers Dogen speaks of here are not the mountains and rivers of the poet, the naturalist, the hunter, the woodsman. They are the mountains and rivers of the dharmadhatu, the dharma realm.

Mountains and rivers are generally used in Buddhism to denote samsara—the world of delusion, the pain and suffering of the world, the ups and downs of phenomenal existence. What we have here is not a sutra about mountains and rivers in that sense, but the revelation of the mountains and rivers themselves as a sutra, as a teaching.

The river Dogen speaks of is the river of the Dharmadhatu, the phenomenal realm, the realm of the ten thousand things. Rivers, like mountains, have always had a special spiritual significance. A lot of spiritual history has unfolded along the banks of the Ganges in India, and on the Yangtse River of China. Much of the dharma and the teachings of Christianity and Judaism have emerged on the banks of rivers.

Thoreau said of the Merrimack River:

There is an inward voice that in the stream sends forth its spirit to the listening ear, and in calm content it flows on like wisdom, welcome with its own respect, clear in its breast like all these beautiful thoughts. It receives the green and graceful trees. They smile in its peaceful arms.

In Hermann Hesse's book *Siddhartha*, the river plays the key role in Gautama's awakening. For me, that book was a very powerful teaching. When I returned to it many years after originally studying it in school, I remember how troubled that time of my life was. Somehow, this book had not sunk in when I was younger. But at this later time, the reading of *Siddhartha* brought me to the Delaware River. Going to the river became a pilgrimage for me, a place to go to receive the river's spirit, to be nourished. I didn't know what was going on, but I was moved by what Hesse had to say about Siddhartha and the river. Each time I went to the Delaware, it was like a clear, cool, refreshing drink of water, soothing a fire inside me. I didn't understand, but I kept going back. I photographed the multiplicity of the river's faces and forms revealed at different times. I found myself traveling the river, immersing myself in it. This went on for years, and for years the river taught me. Then, finally, I heard it. I heard it speak. I heard what it was saying to Siddhartha, and to Thoreau.

In Hesse's story, Siddhartha is in great pain and misery. He wanders in the forest, and finally comes to a river—the river that earlier in the book a ferryman had taken him across. In Buddhist imagery that river and that crossing over is the *prajña paramita*, the perfection of wisdom: "Go, go, hurry, cross over to the other side." We can understand that crossing over in many ways. We can

understand the other shore as being none other than this shore. We can also understand that the other shore crosses over to us, as well as that we cross over to the other shore.

At this point in the novel Hesse writes of Siddhartha:

With a distorted countenance he stared into the water. He saw his face reflected and spat at it. He took his arm away from the tree trunk and turned a little, so that he could fall headlong and finally go under, bent, with closed eyes towards death. Then, from a remote part of the soul, from the past of his tired life he heard the sound. It was one word, one syllable, which without thinking he spoke instinctively. The ancient beginning and ending of all Brahmin prayers, the holy 'Om,' which had the meaning of the Perfect One, or perfection. At that moment, when the sound of Om reached Siddhartha's ears, his thundering soul suddenly awakened, and he recognized the folly of his action.

Hesse goes on for several pages describing the further teachings of the river, and then writes:

I will remain by this river, thought Siddhartha. It is the same river which I crossed on my way to town. A friendly ferryman took me across. I will go to him. My path once led from his hut to a new life which is now old and dead. He looked lovingly into the flowing water, into the transparent green, into the crystal lines of its wonderful design. He saw bright pearls rise from the depths, bubbles swimming on mirror, sky blue reflected in them. The river looked at him with a thousand eyes, green, white, crystal, sky blue. How he loved this river! How it enchanted him! How grateful he was to it! In his heart, he heard the newly awoken voice speak. And it said to him, 'Love this river, stay by it, learn from it.' Yes, he wanted to learn from it. He wanted to listen to it. It seemed to him that whomever understood this river and its secrets, would understand much more, many secrets, old secrets.

Master Dogen addresses the secrets of the river and of all water: *"The river is neither strong nor weak, neither wet nor dry, neither moving nor still, neither cold nor hot, neither being nor non-being, neither delusion nor enlightenment"* It is none of the dualities. Water is H_2O, composed of two parts hydrogen and one part oxygen, two odorless and tasteless gases. You bring them together and you get water. But water is not oxygen, and it is not hydrogen. It is not a gas. It is what D. H. Lawrence calls in one of his poems "the third thing." It is the same way with absolute and relative, with all the dualities. It is not either one or the other; it is always the third thing. The third thing is not strong or weak, not wet or dry, not moving or still, not cold or hot, not being or not-being, not delusion or enlightenment. What is the third thing that Dogen speaks of, that the sutra speaks of, that the river speaks of?

Master Tung-shan is one of the founders of the Soto school of Zen that is part of the tradition of Zen Mountain Monastery. Once when he was crossing the river with Yün-chü, who was his successor in the lineage, he asked Yün-chü, "How deep is the river?" Yün-chü responded, "Not wet." Tung-shan said, "You clod." "How would you say it, Master?" asked Yün-chü. Tung-shan said, "Not dry." Does that reveal the third thing? Is that neither wet nor dry?

Harder than diamond, softer than milk. Harder than diamond expresses the unchanging Suchness of all things, the Thusness of all things. Just this moment! *Softer than milk* refers to the conditioned Suchness of things. Dogen talks in another part of the "Mountains and Rivers Sutra" about the stone woman giving birth to a child in the night. The stone woman is a barren woman and, of course, it is impossible for such a woman to give birth to a child. Dogen goes on to say that this event is "incomprehensible." This refers to the incomprehensibility of something that is without any fixed characteristics whatsoever, without any existence, yet being able to give rise to conditioned existence, to the multiplicity of things. That this is nevertheless true is the basis of the interdependence of the whole universe, what we call the Diamond Net of Indra—totally interpenetrated mutual causality and co-origination. There is no way that you can affect one aspect of this net without affecting the totality of it. With these two phrases *harder than diamond, softer than milk,*

Dogen presents the conditioned and the absolute aspects of reality.

Then Dogen says:

> *We should then study the occasion when the rivers of the ten directions are seen in the ten directions. This is not only a study of the time when humans or gods see the river. There is a study of the river seeing the river. The river practices and verifies the river. Hence, there is a study of the river speaking river. We must bring to realization the path on which the self encounters the self. We must move back and forth along, and spring off from, the vital path on which the other studies and fully comprehends the other.*

What is the path on which the self meets the self, and the other meets the other? It is the practice of the river seeing the river, seeing itself. Dogen expresses it slightly differently in another one of his writings, "Genjokoan." He says, "To study the buddha way is to study the self. To study the self is to forget the self. And to forget the self is to be enlightened by the ten thousand things." When you study the self, you begin to realize that it is a self-created idea. We create it moment to moment. We create it like we create all the ten thousand things, by our interdependency and our co-origination. What happens when the self is forgotten? What remains? The whole phenomenal universe remains. The whole dharmadhatu remains. That's what it means, "To forget the self is to be enlightened by the ten thousand things." That is, we see the ten thousand things as our own body and mind. In one of his poems Master Tung-shan talks about the old grandmother looking in the mirror seeing her reflection. "Everywhere I look, I meet myself. It is at once me, and yet I am not it." You and I are the same thing, but I am not you and you are not me. Both of those facts exist simultaneously, but somehow that doesn't compute. Our brains can't deal with it. The two things seem mutually exclusive. That's why practice is so vital. You need to see it for yourself, and see that words don't reach it. There is no way this reality can be conveyed by words, any more than the taste of the crystal clear water can be conveyed in any other way than by tasting it.

The morning dew on the tips of the ten thousand grasses reveals the truth of all the myriad forms of this great earth. Each thing, each tip of grass, each dewdrop, each and every thing throughout the whole phenomenal universe contains the totality of the universe. That's the truth of the myriad forms of this great earth.

The sounds of the river valley sing the eighty-four thousand hymns of Suchness. Have you heard them? The songs don't just say Om. They sing the eighty-four thousand hymns, the eighty-four thousand *gathas,* the teachings, the sermon of rock and water. Pervading throughout these sounds and forms is a trail far from words and ideas. Have you found it? If you wish to enter it, simply look and listen. But look with the whole body and mind. See with the whole body and mind. Listen and hear with the whole body and mind, and then you'll understand them intimately. That's the entry. If you go chasing it, you won't find it. "To carry the self forward and realize the ten thousand things is delusion," as Master Dogen said. "That the ten thousand things advance and

realize the self is enlightenment." You see? The other shore arrives.

What does it mean that *the river practices and verifies the river?* It means that you practice and verify yourself, and in so doing, it is the practice and verification of all buddhas, past, present, and future. Supposedly Buddha predicted that there will be a time when Buddhism will disappear from the face of the earth. He defined that time as a time in which there would be no masters alive, no sutras, nobody sitting zazen, no realized beings. He characterized it as a time of great darkness, supposedly sometime in the future. Let's say that that time of great darkness has appeared. Let's say it goes on for five hundred years. In such a case one would have to wonder about the mind-to-mind transmission. Even now there are historical gaps in the mind-to-mind transmission. From the point of view of the lineage, we chant the lineage list as though it were a continuum. In Chinese culture there was a great need for ancestral continuity. If there was no legitimate ancestor, they would take a likely name and splice it in, and everybody was happy. Nowadays historians sometimes find out that these names are not the proper successors. And the scholars say, "Aha! mind-to-mind transmission doesn't exist. This teacher died and a hundred years later this other teacher who supposedly got mind-to-mind transmission from him, was just born. There was no mind-to-mind transmission." That's why they're scholars! From the point of view of the dharma, if mind-to-mind transmission disappeared from the face of the earth for a million years, one person doing zazen, realizing the true self, would have the same realization of the buddhas of the past, and the gap of a million years would be filled in an instant, mind-to-mind.

It is as if electricity disappeared from the face of the earth and someone, a billion years from now, created a generator, started turning it, and coiled a wire and attached it to the generator; the more they turned the hotter the wire would get until finally it glowed and light appeared. It would be the same light now produced by lightbulbs, the same electricity. All they would have to do is to produce the electricity. In the case of the buddhadharma, all that needs to be done is to realize it. What do you realize? What you realize is that buddha mind has always been there. You do not attain it, you were born with it. Zen did not come to America from Japan; it was always here, and will always be here. But like the lightbulb, electricity itself is not enough. You need to plug in the bulb to see the light. In the dharma you plug in people; the buddhadharma shines through humans, through Buddhas. Only buddhas can realize Buddha. Dogen says that when we realize Buddha: *"We must bring to realization the path on which the self encounters the self. We must then move back and forth along, and spring off from, this living path on which one studies and fully comprehends other."*

One of the characteristics of the Third Rank of Tung-shan is maturity of practice, emptiness functioning as the basis of daily activity. This functioning is none other than the ten thousand hands and eyes of great compassion—Kannon Bodhisattva. She always manifests according to circumstances. In her manifesting there is no sense of separateness. The realization of seeing our own face everywhere we look becomes action. Not just seeing or knowing our own faces, our true selves, but

Compassion

acting on the basis of this knowledge. This is called the action of non-action. Compassion is not the same as doing good, or being nice. Compassion functions freely, with no hesitation, no limitation. It happens with no effort, the way you grow your hair, the way your heart beats, the way you breathe, the way your blood circulates, or the way you do all the ten thousand other things you do moment to moment. It does not take any conscious effort. Someone falls, you pick them up. There is no sense of doer, or what is being done. There is no separation.

If you want your practice to manifest in the world, if you want to help heal this great earth of ours which is groaning in sickness, you need to realize what we've been talking about. All you need to do to realize it is listen, and through the hum of the distant highway, you can hear the thing itself, the voice of the river. Can you hear it? That's it . . . Is that the third thing?

SACRED WILDNESS

THE RIVER NEVER SPEAKS, *yet it knows find its way to the Great Ocean. The mo have no words, yet ten thousand things are born here. Where the river finds its way, you can perceive the essence. Where the mountain gives birth to the ten thousand things, you can realize the action. When the mind moves, images appear. Even if the mind does not move, this is not yet true freedom. You must first take off the blinders and set down the pack if you are to enter the sacred space. When you let go, even river rocks and brambles are radiant. When you hold on, even the* mani *jewel loses its brilliance. When you neither let go nor hold on, you are free to ride the clouds and follow the wind.*

Buddha said, "All things are ultimately liberated. They have no abode." To say they have "no abode" means they have no resting place, no permanence. One of the characteristics of all things is that they are in a constant state of becoming. Everything is empty of fixed characteristics. And "empty of fixed characteristics" in itself is freedom or liberation.

To say there is no fixed place is just another way of saying that all things are empty. How can that be? What does it mean to be "empty?" Usually when we use that word in our western culture, it implies vacancy, the void. When the word is used in Buddhism it has a different connotation—it means empty of independent being. That is, to be *interdependent* is precisely the same as to be "empty." To recognize one's body and mind as the body and mind of the whole universe, of the mountains and rivers themselves, is to realize the emptiness of all things. It is because things are empty that they can abide in their own dharma state.

"Freedom" and "liberation" are interesting words. Freedom is defined in the dictionary as being "free from bondage or restraint." Liberation is understood in Buddhism as implying "no hindrances, a state of perfection and completion." Gary Snyder, in his book *The Practice of the Wild*, studies and plays with the word "wild," uncovering its many intriguing dimensions and relationships. Drawing from the *Oxford English Dictionary*, he says that when the word "wild" is used in speaking of animals, it means "not tamed, undomesticated, or unruly"; of plants, "not cultivated"; of land, "uninhabited"; of food crops, "yielded without cultivation"; of societies, "uncivilized, resisting government"; of individuals, "unrestrained, loose"; of behavior, "destructive, cruel" or "artless, free, and spontaneous."

Snyder suggests that if we look at "wildness" not from a negative point of view, what it's not, but rather from a positive point of view, we come up with a very different appreciation. In terms of plants, we have "self-propagating and self-maintaining"; of land, "a place where the original and potential vegetation and fauna are intact," or "pristine." In terms of food crops, the positive definition is "food supplies made available and sustainable by the natural excess and exuberance of wild plants in their growth." Of societies: "societies that grow from within and are maintained by a consensus and custom, rather than by explicit legislation." Of individuals: "following local customs, style, and etiquette." Of behavior: "fiercely resisting oppression, confinement, or exploitation. Unconditioned, expressive, physical, and open." When you look at those definitions, you realize that the word "wild" and the word "free" have a great deal in common. In fact, you can even take it further and say that the words "wild," "free," and "nature" are very similar to what we call the "Tao," or the "Way," or the "buddha-nature," or even "sacredness."

We discover during our explorations of the mountains and rivers, that the wilderness can be a tough teacher. A rabbit gets only one chance to run across an open field without first looking up. There is no second chance. That's the way the wilderness teaches. That's the way the insentients teach. Gary Snyder says, "For those who would seek directly by entering the primary temple of wilderness, the wilderness can be a ferocious teacher, rapidly stripping down the inexperienced or the careless. It's easy to make the mistakes that will bring one to an extremity. Practically speaking, a life that is vowed to simplicity, appropriate boldness, good humor, gratitude, unstinting work and play, and lots of walking brings us close to the actually existing world and its wholeness." The wilderness is at once a difficult teacher, and at the same time an open doorway to all in this great earth that we hold sacred. Snyder also says that people of the wild rarely seek out adventures. If they deliberately risk themselves, it is for a spiritual rather than economic reason, and definitely not for the purpose of just simply "getting a rush." The wilderness is filled with rushes; you don't have to create them.

We tend to think of the wild, the free, as being somehow far removed. We'll find it, we think, in the tundra, or deep in the forest, or high on the mountains. But in actual fact, we're surrounded and interpenetrated by wildness, regardless of where we live, whether in the city or the country. The mice in the pantry, the roaches in the wall, the deer on the turnpike—they each exist in the wilderness. The pigeons, the spiders, the bacteria on our skin, in our bodies—they are all free, wild, uncultivated, and unrestrained. The body itself is wild; certain aspects of us, our reflex actions, are manifestations of no mind, no effort. They just respond according to circumstances.

The mind is also free and wild. This free and wild mind includes two domains, though we tend to see only one side: the monkey mind that we sit with. The other side is very still, quiet, open, and receptive. It is not reflective, analyzing, or judging each thing. It simply sees with the whole body and mind, hearing with the whole body and mind. Non-abiding mind is central to all of Zen practice, including the practice of the wild. The minute you fix and reflect on something, you engage the biocomputer, and it takes you away from the moment. That's where we spend most of our time: preoccupied with the past, or preoccupied with the future, while the moment constantly in front of us is barely seen or heard or felt or tasted or touched.

"All things are ultimately liberated. They have no abode." What kind of state is the state of no abode? How can the Buddha make the statement "have no abode" and not be contradicting Master Dogen when he says, "We should realize that although they are liberated, without any bonds, all things are abiding in their own Dharma state." Isn't that referring to an "abode?" Abodes happen when you separate yourself from things. When you realize the whole phenomenal universe as this body and mind, how can there be an abode? It is because all things are ultimately liberated and have no abode that we can say they abide in their own dharma state. In other words, each thing is just as it is.

Buddha, in saying, "All things are ultimately liberated," opens up the trail for everyone. How can you miss it? The Way has no edges. Usually when we think of a path, we think of a clear-cut trail that's been etched out of the wilderness. But the Way that the Buddha opens encompasses the whole thing. It's not something etched out. There is no "this is on the trail and that is off the trail." The whole catastrophe is the trail, and the self. It reaches everywhere. But, if it reaches everywhere, how can we call it a Way or a path?

Buddha's statement, "They have no abode," should not be taken as an abode of no abode, a resting place. People inevitably make a nest here. This is precisely what happens when we attach to non-attachment, when we cling to emptiness. We create two things: the thing held on to and oneself. There's no intimacy there.

An ancient Zen saying goes, "In the beginning, mountains are mountains and rivers are rivers. Then after much study and reflection and going very deeply into oneself, one finds that mountains are many things, and rivers are many things, reaching everywhere, encompassing the whole universe. And then, many years later, the mountains are mountains and rivers are rivers." We should understand that "mountains are mountains and rivers are rivers" as seen by the novice, and "mountains are mountains and rivers are rivers" as seen by the sage depict different ways of seeing. The novice doesn't see the sage's mountains and rivers, but the sage's view definitely includes the novice's mountains and rivers.

The "Mountains and Rivers Sutra" of Master Dogen is not a sutra about mountains and rivers, but the expression of the mountains and rivers themselves as the sutra, as the teaching, as the Buddha, as this very body and mind.

When people look at water, they see it only as flowing, without rest. This flow takes many forms and our way of seeing is just the one-sided

human view. Water flows over the earth. It flows across the sky. It flows up, it flows down. It flows around bends, into deep abysses. It mounts up to form clouds, it descends to form pools.

The teachings of the insentient deal with intimacy, not with words. The teaching is not communicated by words, and yet it is intelligent. And how it communicates! Consider how impossible it is to walk through the forest without telegraphing your presence. Your movements are felt and relayed by all the birds and beasts. The crow tells it to the jay, and the jay expresses it to the kingfisher and the duck and the deer. Sitting in my camp, when neighboring campers walk back and forth, I am aware of their whereabouts, listening to the forest. As soon as they enter the woods on the far side, within seconds the message that they are on their way is passed through the little patch of woods. And all the animals understand it, even my very domesticated dog. Immediately he perks up and looks in the direction of the sounds. He waits for a visual sighting or a scent before starting his racket, barking and carrying on. Isn't that communication? Isn't that intelligence?

When you stop cultivation, even for a very short period of time, the wildness returns. That wildness is akin to the buddha-nature. Civilization has a way of making wildness seem very negative. Yet, all things return to the wild: people, mountains, rivers, gardens, apples, the family cat. It doesn't take long. To be truly free, to be truly liberated and wild, is to be prepared to accept things as they are, abiding in their own dharma state. Sometimes it's painful. And yet, it's also joyful and open. Always impermanent, never fixed. Unbounded, yet bountiful.

Keep in mind that in a fixed universe, there can be no freedom. So, in a sense, we can say that mountains are the entire dharma realm. In those words we include everything. Rivers are the entire dharma realm. They permeate the ten directions. The self is the entire dharma realm. When Master Dogen speaks of mountains and rivers, they're not the mountains and rivers of the poet or the naturalist. They're not the mountains and rivers of nirvana or samsara. They're the mountains and rivers of the true dharma.

To realize the great river is to realize the Three Treasures: the Buddha, the Dharma, and the Sangha. It is to realize the Precepts. To realize these mountains and rivers is to realize every koan, to free oneself of birth and death. This is true not only when we realize mountains and rivers, but when we realize a single drop of water. In it are countless universes. Do you understand? In a single drop of water the entire dharma realm, the whole phenomenal universe exists. Isn't it incredible? You are the entire dharma realm: not just a drop of water, or mountains and rivers, or wise ones and sages. That being the case, what separates heaven from hell? What separates anger from wisdom; greed from compassion? Surface and edge, inside and outside, flowing and not flowing, walking and not walking? What is the cause of that separation? A thought. A single thought and heaven and earth are a million miles apart. How can we avoid the thought? How can we avoid thinking? One great master said, "By thinking non-thinking." When there's not a single thought, then what? What do you do next? Get rid of it. "Not a single thought" is another thought; throw it away.

In the multitude of forms and the myriad appearances, there is not a single thing. Unless you've separated yourself from the myriad things. When there is intimacy, when there is no separation, there is no thing. Mountains and rivers are not seen in a mirror. In other words, they are not seen through a reflection, but directly. How do you see directly? What happens when you see directly?

We spend a lot of time in our zazen working on the internal dialogue that separates us from things. We then take it and work on it in the midst of activity: in our work practice, in our body practice, in the arts of Zen. It's the same way we understand the functioning of the mind: on one side, stillness; on the other side, activity.

In Zen, we start from the premise of original perfection. Each one of us is perfect and complete, lacking nothing. Then on top of that, through a lifetime of conditioning, we pile on all sorts of definitions and habitual behaviors. We pick up all kinds of baggage and create all kinds of blinders. What our Zen practice is about is simply returning to the ground of being. It's always been there. You're born with it, you'll die with it—whether you realize it or not. You can use it, if you realize it.

The process of realization is basically a process of clearing away the extra and getting to that place that's the heart, light, and spirit of each one of us. What you see at that point is the freedom that was always there, the nature that was always there, just wanting to come to the surface, just wanting to express itself.

The ancient wolf caves on Tremper Mountain
Have long been empty.
Yet wolf howls echo in the river valley with each
    winter's full moon.
Some say they are the sounds of the wind
    on the cliffs, or coy-dogs.
Others say, clearly this is the sound
    of the mountain wolf
Have you heard them?

If you want to hear them, you have to listen with the eye and see with the ear. Only then will you really understand. Only then will you really hear the teachings of the insentient. Only then will you hear the sermon of rock and water, the teachings of mountains and rivers.

APPENDIX

The Buddhist precepts are a teaching on how to live our lives in harmony with the totality of the universe. When we look at the precepts, we normally think of them in terms of people. Indeed, most of the moral and ethical teachings of the great religions address relationships among people. But these precepts do not exclusively pertain to the human realm. They are talking about the whole universe, and we need to see them from that perspective if we are to benefit from what they have to offer and begin healing the rift between ourselves and the universe.

The Three Pure Precepts, *Not creating evil, Practicing good,* and *Actualizing good for others,* are a definition of harmony in an inherently perfect universe, a universe that is totally interpenetrated, codependent, and mutually arising. But the question is: How do we accomplish that perfection? The Ten Grave Precepts point that out. Looking at the Ten Grave Precepts in terms of how we relate to our environment is a step in the direction of appreciating the continuous, subtle, and vital role we play in the well-being of this planet—a beginning of taking responsibility for the whole catastrophe.

The first grave precept is *Affirm life—do not kill*. What does it mean to kill the environment? It's the worst kind of killing. We are decimating many species. There is no way that these life forms can ever return to the earth. The vacuum their absence creates cannot be filled in any other way, and such a vacuum affects everything else in the ecosystem, no matter how infinitesimally small it is. We are losing species by the thousands every year—the last of their kind on the face of this great earth. And because someone in South America is doing it, that doesn't mean we're not responsible. We're as responsible as if we are the one who clubs an infant seal or burns a hectare of tropical forest. It is as if we were squeezing the life out of ourselves. Killing the lakes with acid rain. Dumping chemicals into the rivers so that they cannot support any life. Polluting our skies so our children choke on the air they breathe. Life is nonkilling. The seed of the Buddha grows continuously. Maintain the wisdom life of Buddha and do not kill life.

The second grave precept is *Be giving—do not steal.* "Do not steal" means not to rape the earth. To take away from the insentient is stealing. The mountain suffers when you clear-cut it. Clear-cutting is stealing the habitat of the animals that live on the mountain. When we overcut, streams become congested with the sediments that wash off the mountain slopes. This is stealing the life of the fish that live in the river, of the birds that come to feed on the fish, of the mammals that come to feed on the birds. Be giving, do not steal. The mind and externals are just thus, the gate of liberation is open.

The third grave precept is *Honor the body—do not misuse sexuality.* Honor the body of Nature.

When we begin to interfere with the natural order of things, when we begin to engineer the genetics of viruses and bacteria, plants and animals, we throw the whole ecological balance off. Our technological meddling affects the totality of the universe, and there are karmic consequences to that. The three wheels: body, mind, and mouth; greed, anger, and ignorance are pure and clean. Nothing is desired. Go the same way as the Buddha, do not misuse sexuality.

The fourth grave precept is *Manifest truth—do not lie.* One of the very common kinds of lying that is popular these days is called greenwashing. Greenwashing is like whitewashing—it pretends to be ecologically sound and politically correct. You hear Monsanto Chemical Company tell us how wonderful they are and how sensitive they are to the environment. Exxon tells us the same thing. The plastics manufacturers tell us the same thing. Part of what they are saying is true. You couldn't have a special pump for failing hearts without plastic. You couldn't have an oxygen tent without plastic. Sure, fine, thank you. But stop making plastic cups and plates that are not biodegradable

and are filling up the dumps. Another kind of lying is the lying that we do to ourselves about our own actions. We go off into the woods, and rather than take the pains to haul out the nonbiodegradable stuff that we haul in, we hide it. We sink the beer cans, bury the cellophane wrappings under a root. We know we have done it, but we act as if it didn't happen. Gain the essence and realize the truth. Manifest it and do not lie.

The fifth grave precept is *Proceed clearly—do not cloud the mind.* Do not cloud the mind with greed, do not cloud the mind with denial. It is greed that is one of the major underlying causes of pollution. We can solve all the problems. We have all the resources to do it. We can deal with our garbage, we can deal with world hunger, we can deal with the pollution that comes out of the smokestacks. We have the technology to do it, but it is going to cost a lot of money, which means that there will be less profit. If there is less profit, people will have to make do with a little bit less, and our greed won't let us do that. Proceed clearly, do not cloud the mind with greed.

The sixth grave precept is *See the perfection— do not speak of others' errors and faults.* For years we have manicured nature because in our opinion nature didn't know how to do things. That manicuring continues right here, on the shores of our river. We have concluded that the river is wrong. It erodes the banks and floods the lowlands. It needs to be controlled. So we take all the curves out of it, line the banks with stone, and turn it into a pipeline. This effectively removes all the protective space that the water birds use to reproduce in, and the places where the fish go to find shelter when the water rises. Then the first time there is a spring storm the ducks' eggs and the fish wash downstream into the Ashokan Reservoir and the river is left barren. Or we think there are too many deer, so we perform controlled genocide. Or the wolves kill all the livestock, so we kill the wolves. Every time we get rid of one species, we create an incomprehensible impact and traumatize the whole environment. The scenario changes and we come up with another solution. We call this process wildlife management. What is this notion of wildlife management? See the perfection, do not speak of nature's errors and faults.

The seventh grave precept is *Realize self and other as one—do not elevate the self and put down others.* Do not elevate the self and put down nature. We hold a human-centered notion of the nature of the universe and the nature of the environment. We believe God put us in charge, and we live out that belief. The Bible confirms that for us. We live as though the universe were spinning around us, with humans at the center of the whole picture. We are convinced that the multitude of things are there to serve us, and so we take without any sense of giving. That is elevating the self and putting down nature. In this universe, where everything is interpenetrated, codependent, and mutually arising, nothing stands out above anything else. We are inextricably linked and nobody is in charge. The universe is self-maintaining. Buddhas and ancestors realize the absolute emptiness and realize the great earth. When the great body is manifested there is neither inside nor outside. When the dharma body is manifested there is not even a single square inch of earth on which to stand. It swallows it. Realize self and other as one. Do not elevate the self and put down nature.

The eighth grave precept is *Give generously—do not be withholding.* We should understand that giving and receiving are one. If we really need something from nature, we should vow to return something to nature. We are dependent on nature, no question about it. But there is a difference between recognizing dependency and entering it consciously and gratefully, and being greedy. Native Americans lived amid the plenty of nature for thousands of years. They fed on the buffalo when they needed that type of sustenance. We nearly brought that species to extinction in two short decades. It wasn't for food. Tens of thousands of carcasses rotted while we took the skins. It is the same with our relationship to elephants, seals, alligators, and countless others. Our killing has nothing to do with survival. It has nothing to do with need. It has to do with greed. Give generously, do not be withholding.

The ninth grave precept is *Actualize harmony—do not be angry.* Assertive, pointed action can be free of anger. Also, by simply being patient and observing the natural cycles, we can avoid unnecessary headaches and emotional outbreaks. Usually we will discover that the things we think get in the way are really not in the way. When the gypsy moths descended in swarms one year and ate all the leaves off the trees so that in the middle of June the mountain looked as if it were in late autumn, the local community got hysterical. We made an all-out attack. Planes came daily and sprayed the slopes with chemicals. People put tar on the bases of trees to trap the caterpillars. The gypsy moths simply climbed up, got stuck in the tar, and piled up, so that others crawled across the backs of the dead ones and went up the trees to do what they needed to do. Amid all of these disasters, with the leaves gone and the shrubbery out of the shade, the mountain laurel bloomed as it had never bloomed before. I had no idea we had so much mountain laurel on this mountain. However, the gypsy moths definitely damaged the trees. The weak trees died. By the time July came around, there were new leaves on the trees, and the mountain was green again. But the anger and the hate

we felt during those spring months was debilitating and amazing. The air was filled with it.

In another incident, the fellow who owned the house that is now the monastery abbacy had beavers on his property. They were eating up his trees, so he decided to exterminate them. A neighbor told him that they were protected, so he called the Department of Environmental Conservation. The authorities trapped and removed the animals. When we moved into the house, however, a pair of beavers showed up and immediately started taking down the trees again. In fact, they chomped down a beautiful weeping willow that my students presented to me as a gift. I was supposed to sit under it in my old age, but now it was stuck in a beaver dam, blocking up the stream. With the stream dammed, the water rose and the pond filled with fish. With the abundance of fish, ducks arrived. That brought in the fox and the osprey. Suddenly the whole environment came alive because of those two beavers. Of course, they didn't stay too long because we didn't have that much wood, so after two seasons they moved on. Nobody was taking care of the dam. The water leaked out and the pond disappeared. It will be like that until the trees grow back and the next pair of beavers arrive. If we can just keep our fingers out of it and let things unfold, nature knows how to maintain itself. It creates itself and defines itself, as does the universe. And, by the way, the weeping willow came back, sprouted again right from the stump. It leans over the pond watching me go through my cycles these days.

The tenth grave precept is *Experience the intimacy of things—do not defile the Three Treasures.* To defile is to separate. The Three Treasures are this body and the body of the universe, and when we separate ourselves from ourselves, and from the universe, we defile the Three Treasures.

If you don't understand these precepts, study and practice them carefully—practice them with the whole body and mind. This is the key of Zen training. We all have a habitual way of dealing with the world, a way that is self-centered, that comes from our conditioning. This practice is an opportunity to turn it over and see it from all sides, an opportunity to take care of the things that need taking care of in a way that's not self-centered, that doesn't set *this* against *that,* but sees the whole universe as an interacting totality that affects everything. It's only in this way that we can nourish and heal ourselves and the environment.

The precepts are about creating activity in the world in a way that is in harmony with it. It is what we call compassion. The first realization of unity is wisdom, the realization of oneness. The manifestation of that wisdom in the world of separation is compassion, which is the functioning of the precepts.

The bottom line is that these precepts are yours, and no one else's. Please practice them well. In so doing, you take care of this magnificent, great earth of ours. And that is no small thing.

PHOTOGRAPH CREDITS

BOOKS BY JOHN DAIDO LOORI

Cave of Tigers: The Living Zen Practice of Dharma Combat
A one-of-a kind record of what genuine Zen training can be within
the context of an enlivening teacher-student relationship. Culled
from formal public meetings over fifteen years, these transcripts
convey the excitement and seriousness of practicing on the sharp
edge of our self-exploration, with all of its associated rawness, vul-
nerability, spontaneity, and wonder. The book shows that Zen is
alive and well here in America at the turn of the millennium, that
it is accessible to all of us, and that it is completely relevant to the
ways we live our lives. It is an invitation and a map to exuberant
sanity.

Finding the Still Point: A Beginner's Guide to Zen Meditation
Beginner's instruction in zazen, seated Zen meditation. A guide to
discovering the inherent stillness of mind. This book is beautifully
and helpfully illustrated.

Hearing with the Eye: Photographs from Point Lobos
John Daido Loori's stunning array of images taken at Point Lobos,
California beautifully complements his commentary on Master
Dogen's *Teachings of the Insentient,* a profound exploration of the
mystical reality of the insentient. The words and images presented
in this book are an attempt to enter the hidden universe of the insentient and see "things for what else they are." They are an invitation to discover the full spectrum of the teachings of rocks, mountains, rivers, and trees.

Making Love with Light:
Contemplating Nature with Words and Photographs
Brings together Daido Loori's talents as an award-winning photographer and Zen teacher. The essays, images, and poems on these pages fill the gap that separates us from ourselves, and from all that is wild, free, and uncultivated. They are an expression of love using light. Seventy-five full-color plates with accompanying Zen poems form a panoramic vista of and give voice to the mountains, rivers, rock, and sky.

Mountain Record of Zen Talks
Explores Zen practice as a spiritual journey of self-discovery: beginning with the development of a sound appreciation of zazen, realizing the ground of being and the nature of reality, and actualizing these insights in the activities of the world.

Teachings of the Earth: Zen and the Environment
How does Zen practice inform our appreciation of our place in the environment? This book shows us that within stillness is a seed of sanity and a gate to hear the teachings and to heal ourselves. A unique exposition of the awakened ecological consciousness implicit in Zen Buddhism.

Two Arrows Meeting in Mid-Air: The Zen Koan
The definitive volume to koan study and its relevance for modern practitioners. Presents a comprehensive overview of the history and use of koans in Zen training, and contains formal discourses on twenty-one ancient and modern cases. Clearly demonstrates the transformative power of working with koans.